ta(l)king eyes

ta(l)king eyes

Jacque Vaught Brogan

chax 2009

ISBN 9780925904812

Acknowledgments:
The author would like to thank Al Gelpi, Eleanor Cook, and Charles Altieri for their
continued support of all her endeavors the last two decades, as well as the late Margaret
Dickie. She especially wants to thank Cynthia Hogue for her continued spiritual and
poetic encouragement. Parts of this book have appeared in the journals *Joyful Wisdom 2,
Spring: The E.E. Cummings Journal, The Formalist*, and in the one-time publication *More
Than a Whisper* (Univ. of Notre Dame). Thanks to the editors of all of these publications.
The publisher and author also thank the Institute for Scholarship in the Liberal Arts
at the University of Notre Dame for a subvention to help fund the reproduction of
illustrations in this book.

The images used in this book were collected by the author during the time of the writing,
from materials that, as she says, "came to me, uninvited." Their use here is meant to
document this accumulation of magazine pages, newspaper clippings, and postcards,
which relate to, and become part of, the written text of this book.

Published by Chax Press
411 N 7th Ave Ste 103
Tucson Arizona 85705

Printed in the United States of America

for (_____ _____ _____ _____)

and many others

Me talking to me talking to you making eyes
but I confirm it could be about gravel
woman in black which is why I was able to leave (when)
the earth moves too
questioning the history of the objective case—daughters—
two brief lyrics shy and yet another daughter caught it was like i
URANUS/ your anus ***for the children*** INDO-EUROPEAN **
—and one (of crew) and of course it is *the* story,
only in extreme, **the *f* word, fe-, *she,*
How did she get there? Where was she going; the way she does
the target center in her eye *seem*:
ME *semen*; more (mare) at SAME
recipe:
I walked with pounding heart, one more time, prefect perfect/ *mem*
the only sound there is He wrote
but then they would prove
eye-ball
Postscript/Sonnet/ I'll Try a Villanelle
villian:knell/ "who's 'dad' around here"
wonder years the white heat of telling our story not to mention the mirror and the vamp
helio-trope (or only psychologically)
to williams: a reply BASIC BLACK "I" the normative singular pronoun
ta(l)king eyes
passio I want to write
parting to traverse the universe
her/t/s more at he harry/wield really it could be about anything
(t/his gets really fr(i)gtening i'm not mad—really
i'm not MEN MAN quoth the dictionary
indignant decent handsome
joust notre dame why don't you just shut up and take it
grit your teeth and take it like a
tie pin like a flower apologize
dear peter in the waiting room
why we can't speak/why we're never heard

ta(l)king eyes

ME TALKING TO ME TALKING TO YOU
April 20, 2008

Man in White, Woman in Black—Morocco—

MAKING EYES

Man in White, Woman in Black—Morocco

moronic more on it
Good Man. Bad Woman.
clitorectomy
erectomy erect to me

                                        squeeze the silent, the violent
                                        anguish into a   hole. . .

And I can't believe I didn't know infibulation before today.
Convergence of two texts in my life. convergence of two holes
writing over wholes riding over

poreclain bowl. Statue lying on the grass.
Lying. Still. And the figure
on the bed. on the head.
]
                                        Remember (Persephone)

wounded breasts/war/limbs
stuck in vaginas on the cross—

                                        she is not one to whom
                                        these depths are offered.

And the
seduction of being suicidal. Bridal. Bridle.

"All the poets were in love with her."

Want some more nuts?
                         Yes, if you're not going to eat them. I like nuts

And can I enter
the sounding world
without sounding like a good girl/
grand child grandchild sparkling eyes
like Linda (who, of course, for the cute
changed her name to Lynda,
everyone wanting me

to change,
change to Jacqui—insertion of "i"
which is not the I
but object abject *me* me of we(/)ep of waiting for the honor
(it was an honor to dance with
my father/he called me his first part-
ner mom was second)
to be taken home

—as forever
mothers)?

"place where the I endlessly
comes and goes."

Do you have any paper?

    No.

    What Kind?

Any kind.
I'm having a bunch of
ideas and you know
what happens
to those.
having a litter. . .

[and something like grace:
exchanged nuts with one
and like a ghost
generosity moved
to the next seat
delivering this paper

Thanks.
Look at this. . . . I am a professor
at Notre Dame and that experience
makes you sensitive to these things. Of course the *men*
are usually dressed in black.
But I get the picture.

Exercise I:

eye ojo egg/ day's eye daisy/ iris
iris/rising radius/revolving
radiance/at the I
Irving Penn. I arrive
in pen.
penned with your parentheses
(laces, ringed with arrows)

And it's so odd you knowing her, too, and she
with another of the same name.

   "It was violent and destructive."

Me too. So we used to get together and
share stories. So when she asked me, I told her
he's the love of my life
but it would kill me, so I stay
absolutely away.

(seeing only now he was the love
of my death)

And she, the first one ever, *good for you*.
It was such a surprise.

But of course the writing world had agreed
emotion, intensity,
achieved through precise destruction.
And such was cool. Like screwing at parties
on stools, in the kitchen.
But of course it wasn't liberalization
or liberation just the ultimate victory
making us finally flaunt in public
what they'd always taken in secret

I had never understood it really is
you against me.

Naturally when I finally got through,
when I the truth got through
his per-verse vision— women (wo-men)
and me as the supremo cunt—with (her)story,
complaint, he evaporated, a continuing ellipses
taking his parentheses and going home, saying

               I can't do that

that being friends in public

               (twisting)
               I can't do that
               I don't always mean
               to be in control
               but I can't be
               involved (dear
               vulva) in any-
               more destructive
               relationships.
               See: *I* need

It was just like losing MOTHER
M(e enclosed in)OTHER
So
as a note preceding trust
I write this other:
please let me in
I want to talk, to say hexi
Signed Jacqueline
Jacquelinda they said Jacquelindo

BUT I (CONFIRM)
JAC HELENA

—and if, I:
spiced amythest blue
or

ta(l)king eyes

cinnamin silvery crystals in freezing air
or
first fine unfoldings of forsythia—

but then he entered her
in such sweet solution

In the airport like [brackets]
a place of transition [I'll be damned: Pennsylvania] Pen-
cil vania vanitus looking in *The New Yorker*
(Boston, Austin, Houston, Honolulu) to see
if by chance he's there and what kind
of poetry do they let women write anyway answer:
Southern cooking
(and that amazing lifting butterfly going on ahead. . . .)

so that I can finally say it's like this: The blonde,
tanned, blue-eyed, dressed-all-in-black
took my carry-on stay-in-control luggage. Naturally
I was declined
inclined to feel passive but at least
I didn't give her power
of exercising authority
over useless anger—like the other
did (whose uncle Father Sheehy
had just died, from whose funeral
she was returning after, she told me later,
they lost her son's luggage going). So in the airport,
Pittsburg, Pennsylvania I finally buy
my sugar free not-to-feel-guilty candy.
And when I go to pay my billfold
's stuck because everything is packed into
it open. So naturally I say

sorry (meaning I'm dreadfully sorry
for taking up so much of your time)
and she: "I'm not going anywhere.
There's no line behind you."

And I, with the lifting butterfly
say with absolute lilting conviction

it's my lot in life to feel guilty.
And she, as the great farewell:
"why?' I could have kissed her.

So I thought, I've got it: I shall wear my trousers black
and my hair blonde and give them what they wanton want.
it will undo them,
collapsed sacs,
for still I shall enter
on the write: *Job's Daughters*
Dove. Cinnamon. Eye-Shadow.
Calm. Fiery.   Feminine.
It could be about anything.

IT COULD BE ABOUT GRAVEL

And have you ever noticed that

N.B.: and what it really means
in the tradition
of marginality
and who is really writing
when my poetry is dark
like her friend said
"dark, like Plath's?"

                Exercise t/wo:

                for everyone to see
                on the slash
                I in inside
                sword in side

                Exercise t(h)ree:

                and what does it mean
                to be hard as nails
                if the "I" still snails
                like twisting S's inside.

Exercise fo(u)r:

what the eye
must always
        be sEeing
          You at the
deepest   cEnter

No wonder he always tried to enter
or that I spent years
looking for myself in
"you."

Exercise 5/S

        :ymeou
But of course
that's nonsense

"I" marked as absence as
a-post-
rop(h)e

or is i/t
apos-
trop(h)e

WOMAN IN BLACK

what infibulated must look like. and all
for penis (pity).
And look—I can't believe I didn't see
it before (if it was a snake it would have bit me)—
you can see it just starting
to stick through. Man in white.

Morocco. o-rock-o
  petris, petre
   petrified
  peter principle
    principal

Excerc(e)se S(e)x: *17*

the "i"
(i)s not
seen as pal
(i)n principal
(i)n principle

This could really get out of hand.

I learned to hide my pain by entering his. I learned to enter (h)is pa(i)n to avoid mine=
m(i)ne + man = wo-man
And "I" grinning. and how can they
talk like that

                                        putmyhotsteamingchoadin
                                           yourdirttrack

and we/ep had to
like it (being sore
afraid
of what t(he)y might do
if (t)he(y) thought t(he)y could force i/t)

                        Exercise —
                                /:

                        of all the nerve
                        s, members, muscles, bones,

                        organs, hair, tissues,
                        fluids, spaces it is

                        the eye
                        alone
                        which reflects light

WHICH IS WHY I WAS ABLE TO LEAVE

having a mental break down breakdance
breakground—so many parts
of me out there
so many directions
like paralysis—I can't even remember
what all I've written

Exercise e(i)gh(t):

"I" makes all
the difference

between raisin
and Ray's son

between raise son
and raze sin

and so I would write
each wet black as the bond
(for he wanted SEX, the in-
visible
priestess,
wanting (her) touching intelligent
like a beautiful son[g])

beautiful son

with you, boot in my throat,
ich, ich
not to mention
Gretel in darkness all the way
back to Eve
(Aristotle really speaking in lytotes/lies
". . . feminine is a deformity that afflicts half the world."

while the jury is still out de-
liberating (could deformity be a clit grown extra long flagged
turkey skin?)
        it has
certainly been an affliction
     inf(l)ection/infection
in the sentence

                           Exercise n(O)ne:

                           Well, we should be
                           at nine, with none
                           of this stuff we'
                           ve supposedly got past

                           but how can I
                           put the I in—
                           the literal
                           character?—

                           and even if
                           eye can/see I
                           as sound what grammar
                           can i(t) trust as ground

WHEN (THE EARTH MOVES TOO)

what grounds we know
dependent on absence
as center of presence
of which allows plate
movements—and plates—
the event/advent of being
in which all grammar is groundless so I have right to write:
write to right:

ta(l)king eyes

Exercise :-ten

and if "i" is
marked by
apostrophe

what is
S's but
writ-

And something drawn in air
looks exactly like home.
                    Love,
                    (in transition)

/ what the eye cannot hear the ear cannot behold/

and what was the eye anyway
imagio
Iago
iLargo
Key Largo
   (Key West and
ideas of order of
)i

enlarge
improvisations
like this green plant

be/in/side me,
the leaves of which (
long, slender-

ing, pointing
at the end
like a dancer's fingers,

beyond the body's line)

array themselves like a starburst
like aster,

I own not the name of
enlarging like *as*
enlarging like

eyes

QUESTIONING THE HISTORY OF THE OBJECTIVE CASE
—or Bedroom Eyes—

What would it mean to write a sonnet now?
How could we enter that which was inscribed
as *absence* of *we*—women de-scribed—
h(I)erarchy// and *woman* in a shroud?

 Lilacs in bloom are pretty in themselves
(See, how they grow) and dull to all the Gods
though god, s/he, is the light—always the "odd,"
"irrational"—the one which always dwells

from *she* to shining *see*, that should not be
put out, that should not be (woman in black:
infibulated) convicted as lack,
compared to man, as mere deformity

(as Aristotle said—and all fathers
who made [them] bowls, who turned *she* into *her*

—DAUGHTERS—

eyes and I
still don't get it
can't say it

eye nose it
's like i-
ris (trying

ta(1)king eyes

to say I-
are-us or
I rise) yet

erotic
plumage, un-
folding, ex-

foliation
(infibulation)
yellow—with

purple cen-
ter inside
the (lapsed) lips—

or purple, yel-
low center—does
it matter?—

—Want the
flower, yel-
low centered,

(not sin-t(her)ed)

Exercise E(l)even

if you got it
flaunt it

I's got it
I's got it

(eyes got it)

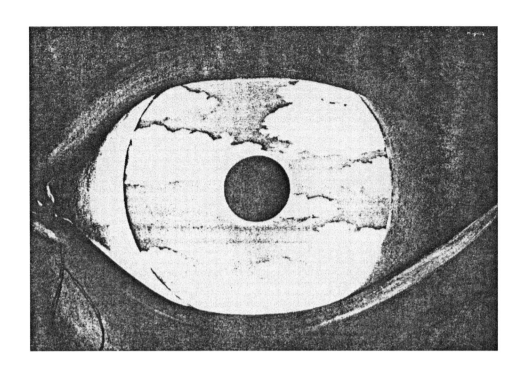

ta(l)king eyes

TWO BRIEF LYRICS SHY
so I ask
if I can ask
(and who is wanting to speak?)

polyphony—like trees singing
through the bird
—clear sound
the form of right sound—

people speaking
not through trees,
but trees through
us—*bopis*
where we play and "I"
everywhere with eyes
for the wonder

and the danger
pounding of paternal
I: "I'll sting
you on the bottom"?

almost like accident:
snake in the flour
boar in the bower

Exercise (T)we(lve)

Eye, the iris,
calm, unfolding
to the light

rainbow,
expanding
horizon

rose, gold
blue to you
as I see

how(ever)
you could
see me—

AND YET ANOTHER (DAUGHTER) CAUGHT—

and does it matter, the names?
that one means "Who is God?"
and the other, merely "son"?—
with the I will change
your clothes, I'll change
your money, your stories
your language—like grafting
plants, forcing flowers—
I am, I seductive, enthralling
for your money, for your
honey. And all to take

your mind as figure,

as interest.

Exercise Thirteen

the tree be-
gins to write—
we keep on

bearing
blooming
like sight

like eyes
released
from blinders

IT WAS LIKE I
disappeared
in that eye

the penis
makes at the tip,
and it was full,

and awful.
exactly as if
t(he)y dotted the (i)

Exercise Thirt(ee)n
I wish to see
and in my husband

the space
the i-

ris opens
rising in

the move-
ment of *as*

as I, as iris,
as ur/us

URANUS/YOUR ANUS

Exercise 1(4)

all—I by
right, by write

Exercise 10+5

When I open
                          my eye to
                          day's eye

what in my
self pulls me

to I or

I to me?
Or is it
I to eye?

Exercise s(e)xt(o)n

Where am I?

      Love, Echo

When did the sun's
day become Son's Day?

****
(sunday) FOR THE CHILDREN:

The leaf of the geranium like its flower,
of different color, so all is connected
if you look carefully enough: three sections,
within each, three scalloped edges.

Multiplicity of color is blessing.
It would be boring if all were green.

And lines looking like fingers of a human
hand.

Trinity in nature
and in humans as I the soul
     me the spirit
     self the dancer
=choreography
"Take turns."

("I think God makes turns to make people understand the world. But sometimes it's
aggravating.")
****

It is *the* story. I don't know of any woman who's made it through without negotiating some sort of sexual time bomb.

I have stories and stories to tell you. . . .

and even after that, they made him chairman.

And the other's now chairman at Harvard.

And the first now edits the most powerful journal in our field. . . . [out filed]

And then the one about the guy calling women
who keep children in their homes
talking dirty about children. So of course
they made him President
of the U.S.A. School of Writing
(women instructors required to take masculine pseudonyms))

Everything connected by "and" and "and"
Everything connected by so and so and so

Exercise Se(v)e(nteen)

In Anglo-Saxon, woman
as chattel, as barter
between lords:

poetic formula—
peace-weaver
(soon dead, like

women in Westerns,
like women in wes-
(s)tern romances

everything connected
by sew and sew

Indo-European —**

from whence derives shirt, skirt
cut, short
itch, scratch
scar, scabies, scabbard

"The law," he says, "can be decon-
structed because it was con-constructed. Justice, if it exists, never."

     Excercise ten+ate

     lan-
     guage
     can

     B   D
     con

     structed
        D con
        stricted

     Ex(o)rcis(m) Nineteen

     To her coming—
     not, let's say
     as pretty as
     a picture.

     This is not, let's say,
     a pretty picture.

She is not
　　　　let's say
　　a pretty
picture (lines
　　already

　　drawn)—let's say

AND ONE (OF CREW
cut, of marine
-s, of full profes-
sor of law) said
to the establishment
of a sexual harrass-
men(t) poliCY: SO
you stand for for-
nication

and the sam(e)
said to the suggestion
of a committee
on the status of wo-
]men at [of course
Notre Dame: SO
you stand for il-
legal murdering
of babies

       Exercise t(win)ty

       she-boom
       she-bang

AND OF COURSE IT IS *THE* STORY, ONLY IN EXTREME

once upon a time, long long ago,
before *man* and *woman* were trapped
as metaphors (woman in black, man in white)
gender was a physical fact

THE HAND AS BEING

In the last moment of the catastrophic momentum,
Too conscious of too many devestations at once,
One man beheld the naked, shameless land

Touched it and wondered: why in the world
Women had seemed mountains in air
To conquer, with spikes and axes, and bare.

Too conscious of too many deaths at once
In the last moment of this escalated momentum,
The land decomposed as it decomposed the sea.

The drying wind scarred the trees, and ah,
It scorched the shrivelling limbs
Then spread its flames over the polluted lakes.

The land decomposed him like a hand seared,
Of an incensed gesture, a woman's hand.
He was too conscious of too many wounds

In the last moment of this ancient momentum.
Her hand took his and drew him near to her.
Her eyes looked on him and the singed dove flew

Across the vast reaches of the garden's end.
Of her, and of the land, at last he knew
And grieved over what could have been, with care.

drawing by Vivienne Padilla

Exercise Twenty-I

In a dark time the I
        begins to C

the see begins to eye

**THE F WORD: FE-
male/feminist/ardent—she who has the ardor to be when i(t) is acutally (evil)/(eve-ill)
OR?
/concerned—she who believes i(t) to be (merely) malignant neglect, redeemable through
learning to see**

Exercise T(win)ty-two

** live here, between your eyes and you,
But ** live in your world. What do ** do?
—Collect no interest—otherwise what ** can;
Above all ** am not that staring man.

SHE:

on one stalled second. She'll consult
not time nor circumstance. She calls

She stands upon her toes and turns and turns.
Above her head she poses

black into white she went
but she was cheerful.

but she never, never smiles)
perhaps she's a daytime sleeper.

she'd tell it to go to hell,
and she'd find a body of water,

she holds but cannot wield,
 She exhibits the talcum powder,

She bends above the other,
Her home, when she is at home, in Glens Fall

exactly as she must have greeted theirs:
She has gone over and over

She thinks that her equinoctial tears
She cuts some bread and says to the child,

She shivers and says she thinks the house
She sits and watches TV.

No, she watches zigzags.
"No," she says. No hope.

She watches on and on,
but she's not a poor orphan.

She has a father, a mother,
and all that, and she's earning

She speaks: "I need a little
She seems to think it's useless

Does she dream of marriage?
Then one day she confides

that she wanted to be a nun
She was a white hen

How did she get there?
Where was she going:

the way she does on other nights,
She leans on the slack trolly wires.

even then I knew she was
She regards us amicably.

what he said, what she said,
She died in childbirth.

She went to the bad.
"Look! It's a she!"

 She drives her gentle children wild
She's picked up many *gourmet** tricks

On stealthy-stealing feet she come again.
And she will slip

/the hugbug
they'll hug you when you feel glad
the hugbug
they'll hug you when you feel sad
the hugbug
they'll hug you when you've been bad/

(not to mention—
selected he

This is a scene where he who treads the boards
he says he

He does not see the moon; he observes only her vast properties,
the moon looks rather different to him. He emerges

He thinks the moon is a small hole at the top of the sky
runs there beside him. He regards it as a disease
he has inherited the susceptibility to. He has to keep
as he stares back, and closes up the eye.

He is the more intelligent by far.
He hung a grunting weight,

He needn't try to make amends,
(Though they say he never raped),

He was all white, like a doll
We talked about the War, and as he cut

away, he croaked out, "Sir, I do declare
He speaks in perfect gibberish

What has he done?
He bounces cheerfully up and down;

he rushes in circles in the fallen leaves.
so much he gave it to me.

/sit silently until he goes,
or else forgets the things he knows./

Exhersighs Twenty-Three

He had 100
years to study
the issues:

"In my life-
time I've
seen this

country dis-
integrate."
Platform:

expects wo-
men to stay
home if they

have children
[Have gun
will travel]

Exercise T(we)nty fo(u)r:

she'll console

when she is at home, is in glands, fall

No, she watches gir(l)gags
then one day she reclines

(they wanted her to be a none)

HOW DID SHE GET THERE? WHERE WAS SHE GOING: THE WAY SHE DOES
on other nights? "When did it get this way? It wasn't like this when I was growing up."

when they grow up, girls enter
the sentence.
infection in the sentence.

       X-her-thighs 2S:

This is a *scene* (Italian: *last supper*)
              where he who threads the broads   the moon looks rather different
to him [in-
              fib-
              u-
              (sxhxe)-
              lation]
                    He emerges
He thinks the moon is a small hole at the top

What has he done?
He bounces cheerfully up and down.

THE TARGET CENTER IN HER EYE/
which eye's his eye?
hold up a flashlight to his eye.
It's all dark
pupil

Exercise Twenty-six:

s(i)gned
(singed)
your pupil

and, still, "They flash upon the inward eye"
(while others flash/flesh upon the wayward eye)

Exercise Twenty s(eve)n:

Daffodil:
French (t)he+
        affodil

akin to OHG *the—*
more at *that* +
        a flower

with a large
corona
        elongated

into a trumpet

deciliter/declit-
crown/corona/cornea

"If what we see could forget us half as easily,"

pillar so the people and the Pope might see

    Exercise Twenty (h)at(e):

    We say, "Come see the jets!"
    We say, "Come see the baby!"
    to see what i(t) was I was.
    with my red berries,

     my (read: buries)
    just to see

From our superior vantage point, we can clearly see

See, up there, pink and plump and smug in sashes,

    Exercise 29:

    intwine
    he says

    (t)hose
    ()nights

. . . she took a thousand stars in her hands and flung them into space (the vast darkness, which is really the shadow of her face)

    Exercise t(her)ty:

    sego: the edible bulb of the lily
    s(h)ego: the edible bloom of the (i)ll
    see: OE, *to say*
    see: ME, *to sit*
    (more at *cathedra*)

seem: ME *semen*; more (mare) at SAME
moronic

more on it
SAME: [ME, fr. ON *samr*;
    akin to OHG *sama* same,
    L. *simulis* like,   *simul* together, at the same time
    sem- one, Gk *homos*, same,   *hama*, together,
    hen-,
    heis, one]

       Exercise 3(1):
        Take the key and lock her up
       lock her up

       look her up
       Take the key

       and lick her up
       my fa(i)r lady

Here we go round the mulberry bush
the mill
(bury us)

       Exercise 32:

       When the circ)us
       comes to town

       I see h(ea)orses
       go round and round

RECIPE:
Cut trimmed
into bite-size cubes
Peel and cut
into
separate
cut into
Slice
Spray large non-stick
Arrange

ta(l)king eyes

Stir
Add
Cover and simmer for 4 or 5 minutes

/cooking skills
to tame/

    Exercise 3-free

    "As for the wines
    buy-at-noon
    uncork-at

    dinner mer-
    chandise," some
    /sum/ may be

    found for less
    at discount
    outlets— —-

    (along with day-
    old bread)

I WALKED WITH POUNDING HEART.
I saw the little pond
I can tell what I saw next; it was not a miracle.
I want to tell you

I'm going to go and take the bus
I think the trees must inter(-)vene

and feel I can't endure it
in a language I didn't know

Exercise 34
all children know
3+4= 34

To meet,
when Eye

meets you—
or Love—

to meet
such eyes

beyond I's
in your eyes

she-boom
she-bang

You can leave your hat on. I know what love is.

X her I's: 35:

just what
you do
to me
do to

me/just
call me

angel
of the

mo(u)rning
baby

ONE MORE TIME

(lost in the poet
's derby:
she critiqued
he published

he wrote
she bit her nails

(Stop. here's
my love

I cannot
speak:

the scream
in palm—

with all
bruises—

the pea.
princess.)

Exercise (th)irty s(e)x

In a dark time the eye begins to see
(Such light, as gleaming black, defiled)
Just what it is. You really do to me

just what you want—like nailing on a tree
the perfect cunt (she really was a child
in a dark time). The eye begins to see

the tribute demanded, bent on the knee
(as faith, beguiled, *myself* filed—
just what it is you really did to me—

when I took your shame (you said it was the key
to unlocking love before you were defiled
in that dark time—before you went sea,

a man lost, trying to prove you are a *he*
/afraid of being *she*/)—before you styled
just what you would really do to me:

you took my words—and all that I could be—
me a hollow skull screaming in the wild
in a dark time. The I begins to see
just what it is you really did to me.

Chain, chain, chain,
chain of fools.

Shame, shame, shame

PREFECT PERFECT

Man in White, Woman in Black
Good Man.   Bad Woman.
Light.   Dark.
Strong.   Weak.
Right.   Wrong.
Governor.   Governess.
Master.   Mistress.

Past Master: an official   Past Mistress: offal

—in the Renaissance, shrine of the huMANities,
from the Middle Ages, shrine of t(HE)ology:
the scold's bridle
(Bride's Scold):
a metal tongue depressant,
locked by head
gear, like a muzzle
like a chastity belt
(infibulation)

ta(l)king eyes

—in OE, no word
for sister (later
borrowed: Scan. *sweoster*);
and *woman* < wif (wife) + man

—and in
L: *meretrix* (prostitute) > meretricious,
also, merit
also, memory,
also, mind

mem: wife of a white British consul

—and has there
(how)ever been
a word for wo-
man that was
not chattel?
(and mouth,
squeezed, as
if by her own
hand, to vulva)?

prolapsed valve > panic
prolapsed vulva > panic
panic < of or relating
    to the male god
     Pan
pa(i)n

    Exercise Thirty-sever

    what if milk
    were not milled

(Irradiated dried milk being sent to Third World—-)

    and if womb
    were not wound

(One-third of all American women to be raped in their lifetime)

    could our gen(i)us
    finally find sound?

THE ONLY SOUND THERE IS
—listening for sound, and staring,

    Exercise 3/8

    two forms
    so much a/like

    one open
    one closed

    why such
    intercourse:

    lacking
    discourse

The Hand as a Being
       X his signs t(her)ty-n(i)ne

      I (right):
      The Hand as Being

I would *turn* (etymos: verb/word/verse)
(he said, the centuries have a way of being masculine)
—BUT THEN THEY WOULD PROVE

      Exercise 4(0)?

      [eccentric. ic. (i)r-
      reconcilable differences

while (I)

      Exercise 4(I)

      for one
      for once
      iris
         Irene
            Eileen
      eye land
      eye lens

Will nature say I told you so
I would tell you if I could

                    This is Jacque Vaught Brogan
                    reporting from Notre Dame

ta(l)king eyes

There ain't nothing like a dame.
Nothing in the world.
There ain't nothing you can name
That is anything like a dame.

"This endlessly elaborating poem"
making eyes
bedroom eyes
it's all in her eyes
the eyes say it all
the eyes have it

Exercise f(our)ty-two

or I^3

I
I am
the one—
I am the power
fierce when broken

Me, I am the song
I sing the fountain,
florescent shower

myself, it is
the dancer

it is through
my self
they find

expression

as the one
      in my self
who dances
     who touches
 I give
as the flower
waving polyp

ta(l)king eyes

                    my-
            self
                        dancing con/
                figurations

                    me—it is the magic
                        of never seeing you
                        in case of object
                    me—it is the magic
                        always seeing
                        you in subject

                    magic where we mingle

                    harmony—

    in—

            choreo-
                graphy—

EYE-BALL
/eye-bolt/eye-catcher/eye-dropper/eye-hole/eye-lid/eye-opener/eye-shot/eye-strain/eye-witness

With the privileging
of the industrial arts,
it was not just
decorative art, but
the liberal arts
which were trivilized
(trivia-lies'd)
trivia [l] eyes

[ta(l)king eyes]

POSTSCRIPT:

Read my lips:
We can't go on this way.
 "Read my lips":
(He *bought* a woman's words!)

Read my lips:
His eyes are in her way.

Read my lips:
Who am I to say?

SONNET:

Angry eyes—that's why they're
     hidden behind veils
Angry eyes—finally darting
     flashing like knives

Hungry eyes—walking backward
     (receding trails)
Hungry eyes—no word for *women*
     that wasn't *wives*

     Ta(l)king eyes—
          how can (s)he ever
          be really heard

     ta(l)king eyes—
          our (w)hole (hi)story
          so damned absurd—

"She really is so well preserved."

I'LL TRY A VILLANELLE
(VILLIAN: KNELL)

I want to say what all it is I know.
Perhaps the "torrid" does make the space to grow.
If such darkness proves the dawning light,

I need to say. But all it is I know
Is simple moonlight arriving through the night.
If you cannot hear, I know not where to go.

If such darkness proves the dawning light,
The dawning of evening promises to show
—above the trees, the stars—that it can write

What I want to say. Yet all it is I know
Is boars among the bowers. (l)awful might
to silence showers. Yet even words could glow

If such darkness proved the dawning light
(Though where I am you still don't want to go).
And if such darkness fails to dawn the light,
How can I say what all it is I know?

"WHO IS DAD AROUND HERE?"
or a lopped/lapsed sestina

One little girl reading by the lamp
Dreams of leaving, going off to camp
Where she can finally escape the stamp
Sent on letters backwards to the damp
House she knew (when trying to climb the ramp
That could erase the label "tramp").

It's no wonder she'd like to tramp
Her home: many eyes like darkened lamps
That (with their silence) blocked the ramp
Of "freedom," "autonomy." (Really, *it's not camp*—
but the heart's chimney with its damp-
er closed—as if this story were engraven stamps.)

CALENDAR

MINNEAPOLIS: through June 18

"Marcel Broodthaers" presents the work of the poet-turned-artist and includes sculptures, paintings, drawings, books, installations, photographs and a retrospective of his films. Broodthaers began making art in the mid-'60s, inspired by American pop artists George Segal and Jim Dine. At the Walker Art Center. (612) 375-7622.

Petite armoire noire avec neuf pots (1965), by Marcel Broodthaers

WASHINGTON: through June 18

"Alfred Stieglitz and His Circle" presents 19 photographs from the "Equivalents," a series of more than 500 images that Stieglitz created between 1921 and 1936. Stieglitz was a pioneer photographer and founder of An American Place. Accompanying the photographs will be paintings by many of the artists whose work and careers were championed by Stieglitz — among them Georgia O'Keeffe, John Marin, Arthur Dove and Marsden Hartley. At the Phillips Collection. (202) 387-2151.

. . . .

She is a tramp now. (So, by others stamped.
It always was damp, a concentration camp.)
She remembers the ramp, like a moving lamp.

WONDER YEARS
Conclusion: May 8, 1990

Your father will always be your father. And he will always leave a light on for you.

      Exersighs: For-he-threes

      From whom? These sigh(t)s
      That worm through just like tears?
       —As if that said it all.

      [while t(ears) tear
       it's certain that tears t(ear)]

      Lies. Crowding e(yes).
      For him to call
      I've waited literal y(ears).

Perhaps they knew that all along.
But it's news to me.
:like escape from Hungary,

the need for verbs,
the need for verse,
(the need *per-verse*):

THE WHITE HEAT OF TELLING OUR STORY

Sunlight splaying
across dark
waters

opening of the
(hollowed) space:
white, hot

black/yellow
the Spirit
has moved through

Exercise 4/4:

Can must i/t
always arrive

the cutting s/lash
—I see the star/

fish flower
turning radiant

"only when our history [(hi)story],
our story, *if*
you will,
has been re-(l)-eased
will we come
into our own
(not sadistically,
not priapistically)
stylistically

Exercise F(our)ty-5:

prismatically: :authority
   as
   (re-
   versed)
genitally: :polyphony

 [mono-
     phony =
 man/me
     phony]

Exercise 4/sicks

 hungry eyes/angry eyes/ta(l)king eyes

NOT TO MENTION THE MIRROR AND THE VAMP:

There once was a girl from Odessa,
who was taught she was *really* Duessa,
While she learned well the part
He ate her whole heart
As an offering to (blank) Fidessa.

". . . each man holds the image in his mind of the perfect virgin
he has whored"

and so Ed (Edward: etymos, *guardian*) says,
It's your curse:
the universal is passing through you.

     Exercise 4 —
          /:

     that/s the question
     can curse be cross be cure?

(it's such temptation
to see this pa(i)n as sanction

On location:
Jacque Vaught Brogan

(not to mention vocation/invocation)
ta(l)king eyes

anaculture: a mixed bacterila culture; *esp*: one used in the preparation of autogenous vaccines

(let not the place of space
be of military installations)

absurd: fr. L. *absurdus*, fr. *ab* + *surdus* (deaf—more at SURD)
   ab: more at OF; from; away; off
   surd: L *surdus* deaf, silent, stupid—more at SWARM
   swarm": = : *hum*

[*eye*— = sight and say]

talk: OE *talu* (tale)

Just the hell's who's talking? whose taling? and who the hell is seeing/ who is saying? who the hell is aye-ing/ who is eyeing? and who the *hell*
? (*etymos*: conceal)

[Absorbing, rather than being absorbed]

Hell:
He thinks that hell rages below his iron feet,
she'd tell it to go to hell

Taking:
See it taking root like weeds,
taking cabs in the middle of the night.

Taking her time.

Talking:
I hear your voices talking.
laughing and talking to hide her tears.
talking, in Eternity:
Talking the way they talked
have ruined it completely. They're just talking.

           just ta(l)king

Hey, some things you just can't say no other way.

way:
give way; they will not bear the weight
some hands point histrionically one way
There is no way of telling.

the way he always painted
all the way to Boston."
Ta(l)king the way they talked

        Coming to you live,
        Jacque Vaught Brogan

Exercise Forty-e(l)ght:

green eye'd
blue eyes

Old Blue Eyes
black eye

Don't it make my brown eyes blue
Single eye

Slant eye
Bull's eye

red eye
(realize)

cyclops/cyesis
real eyes

monster <L. mone're: to warn [*e(r)go*], any woman
who sees poetry everywhere

ta(l)king eyes

HELIO-TROPE: OR (ONLY) PSYCHO-LOGICALLY

                    my   FATher taught me
                                    oo
                    dAnce   w hen 1 was
                    T   0   With
her mother's daytime   Hel **P** and
   husband's evening dutiEs
                    MRsVAught   He called me

            his firsT
                    R d   p
            M w **I** a   a
              o a Attended Sul Ross in 1954 summer
            semesteR   c   t
                    e   i   n
                    C ng   er
                            o
                    H n
                                    d

always an **H**
        t**O**
      da**N**ce with my
        O
  FATHER   . . . left with the sole
      E
      E   care of her
      N   u
                            d
                            d   blonde
                    blonde
                            y   daugh(t)er

SHOULD BE **T**
He
cAn
daNce
K
F
U
L

Jacque Vaught Brogan

    . . . and outside
the cycles of the sun, the endless
changings of the end of day,

the melding blues, belie the cycle
of our nights. There
one keeps his secret in his room—

yet another draws his curtain:
dark womb. And we? who
use words so well? We say

there's nothing by which to tell—
all hearths have cooled. We say
let us open doors in each other

where we can enter, precisely,
such nothingness. (Or SO
we were taught to say.)

      while outside
night marks time's *passus*
with bursts of white
(shooting stars)

    Exercise 4/nun

    "Don't you look nice and red today."
    (Don't you look nice and read.)

      "Oh, you're always dressed so nice.
      Just like a little girl."

    (I/t was a little girl:
      'Look at my outfit')

    could most definitely
    lead to hys-

    terical fits

ta(l)king eyes

"She was in a *fit*"

"She was in a *state*"

ta(l)king eyes

Defining
to refine
and redefine

again
yet never
touching

final
such are we.
We make

our moments,
the great horn
blast of jazz

all to find
again some
wriggling

melody.
I've seen
the sun burn

through the fog:
each wave,
each house,

each leaf
more white
than pierce of

touch or tone
(and yet before
night rain dis-

solve all—
regardless
of us who
tried to make
the moment
an intelligent song

Exercise 5/0
(Or three ways of picturing the cross)

Oh, will the circle be unbroken. . .

TO WILLIAMS: A REPLY

I had a dream
last night about

peaches ripening
because

it was spring.
Forgive me.

They're not lying
in any icebox.

[eye box
black box]
squeeze box

      Exercise 5/(1)

      cauterize?
         cut her i's?

     catheterize?
        cap her eyes?

      catholicize?
       (Catathecize)

BASIC BLACK

woman in black
woman in white
woman in back

ta(l)king eyes

woman in veils
ears pierced
stomachs girdled

waists corseted heels high
feet bound

necks bound
infibulated the
whole world round

She's so reserved.
She never says what she means.
She's so sensitive.
She's just not open.
She can never get to the point.
She talks too much.
She's always whining.
She can't make up her mind.
She's so frigid.
She's a *dog*.
She just yap-yap-yaps.
She gets so hysterical.
(I)t's just her old yackety-yak.

Don't be such a sissy.

(i)/t staggers the (i)mag(i)nation

Exercise 5/for:

map of language:
[(l)anguish]

but of course the assumption *is* girls aren't women until married, until penetrated by a man.

well of course that's *the assumption* and exactly what a man *would* say. but little girls physically become women—if we can define *woman* even in those terms—with their first periods. and girls don't need men (or boys) for that

Exercise f()fty- f()ve:

map of language
ta(l)king eyes

first period.
penetrated

penisized

penal(eyes'd)

daughter *Jessica* (etymos: God is gracious) 3: god speaks jesus everywhere 4: more like myself of course 5: two kinds of real/ this bear is real in this world and I am real in this world and I am alive in reality [save her from a poet's ta(l)king, so ripe for the ta(l)king] 6: I can't figure it out I don't see how anybody could but I *believe* 8: god has to be both, both female and male//son *Evan* (etymos: God is gracious) 3: I see thunder
and lightning in your eyes   4: when you talk
like that I can really see

Exercise Fifty/sicks:

I (I), -pron., nom. 1. the nominative singular prounoun, used by a speaker in   referring to *himself* [italics m(i)ne]

"I" THE NORMATIVE (singular) PRONOUN TA(l)KING EYES

I, 1. the ninth in order or in a series

-i-, the typical ending of the first element of compounds of Latin words, as -o- is of Greek words

I., 1. independent

i., 1. imperator

IAEA
International
Atomic
Energy
Association

IATA
International
Air
Transport
Association

ICA
International
Cooperation
Administration

ICAAAA
Intercollegiate Association of Amateur Athletes of America

ICAO
International Civil Aviation Organization

ibid. ibidem

I. C. Jesus Christ

(I see. Jesus Christ!)

ich:

Exercie 5 (   ):

It's all of a whole
It's all of a hole

It's all of a piece
It's all for a piece

It's so hard, to have passionate *I's* with such
impassioned eyes

and yet I know
there have been such

ta(l)king eyes

richening times
—as if time
opened

and the world looked
deeply round,
so deep each leaf/ deep
the space between each

I know there have been
times when a single strand
of hair (giving, re-
flecting, a panoply
of color
 sparkled blue, red,
brown, yellow, but
mostly sparkling light
have been the actual
strand, connecting

each to each (heart
beating with the sun
the clearing stars,
as if bursting
from their nests—

I know there have
been times when
words were finally
heard/ when the actual
scene = eye to eye

{(/Exercise/)} /)}{(

Rewritten as if in inscribing these lines I could exper-
ience the exquisite joy of dis- covering my own name
Rewritten as if
in inscribing these lines

I could experience
the exquisite joy

of discovering my own name

     Rewritten
           as if in
          inscribing
the lines I
       could exper-

    ience the
            exquisite   joy of dis-
covering

     my own name

Far More Than
(ex) Her eyes, 5 to 9:

As the iris
radiant arrives

through its
own pupil

it seems like
all irises

opening, delicate, flaming

like lilies
bursting

breathing, smelling

like light
expanding

expansive, as if this

were a literal
(multi-verse)

passio—"A passion that we feel, not understand": t(wo) let the pain shine through, to embrace its desire—not as masochistic massacre: the twist of knife: orgasmic spasm—not as unrequited burning in the breasts—but as the actual, actual stone/acutal bread, the truth finally accepted, witness to concrete expansion, like sunlight splaying across dark waters, opening of the hollowed space (white, hot, black/yellow) the Spirit has moved through

Exercise 6T:

matted eyes

(shattered i's)

(scattered i's)
battered eyes

Exercise 6/1

reflecting
upon
reflections

Exercise 6-2

if it's true
that the retina

retains my
image)inverted(,

do the eyes
in the mirror

contain my true
image (reversed)?

X-RAY EYES:) () (

He could look/write/through you

Exercise sixty-fo(u)r:

optic nerve:
optimum blind
spot which makes
all sight
passable

. . . that long corridor I called my childhood was not like a passage at all but more like the ice blue band in the northern winter sky, pressed evenly below furrowed clouds—blank space, flat blue that should mean light and air, but which is simply narrow, cold and sheared—like natural slate

Exercise 60 + 5:

Mon-
u-
men(t)

erected
for
neither

ears
nor
eyes

Exercise 6/6:

Meta-
physical
monthlies

meta-
physical
gulpings

(formless-ness
gulping
after form)

each mouth
(each or(i)face)
a gaping

bl(i)nded eye. . . . .

May 14, 2008: "nobody ever understood what she went through. they just thought she was
ec-
centric
(dis/
playing herself)
shutting herself up
that way

   Don't grimace. Smile, girls. Perhaps if you held up that
   quilt.

       My mother's made 50 qui(l)ts.

   Of course I have. I'm 91 and near my grave.

       Nonsense. You'll live to make
       50 more quilts.

   No I won't. I'm not making any more quilts."

Exercise sixty-(s)even:

and how others
    color

what light we
    bring

myriad mani-
    festations. . .

and how the
    light

first finds each
    f(l)ower

before it turns
    toward. . .

Will history say "that's all she wrote
If brooks and lions should vanish?
And blame the woman for her rape

(The earth defiled with spilling bloods—
"Mother Earth," a hag, worn with use).
Will history say *that's all she wrote*

Though women's words are never heard.
(Though she screamed "NO!"—repeatedly—
They blamed the woman for her rape.)

If AIDS should spread to all our children,
The great lakes turn to mucky sand,
Will (hi)story say "That's all she wrote"?

If she's exploited by reporters
While donning artificial limbs,
Will they blame the *women* for her "rape"?

While the ozone widens exactly like
Every sexual violation,
History still says, "That's all. . . . *She* wrote,"
And blames the "woman" for her rape.

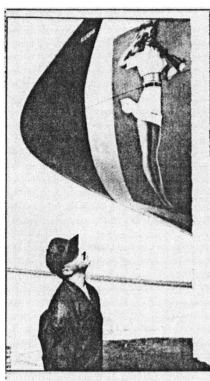

World War II pinups return but updated

CASTLE AIR FORCE BASE, Calif. (AP) — Painting pinups on airplane nose cones, an art form that reached its zenith in World War II, is making a comeback at this Strategic Air Command base.

A KC-135 Stratotanker now sports a 1940s-era calendar pinup, a looker in a midriff and a miniskirt rippling in the breeze.

Castle Air Force officials say the painting is designed to instill pride in the crews that fly and maintain SAC aircraft, but some women's rights groups say they find the pinup art form offensive.

Col. Richard Martin, commander of the 93rd Bombardment Wing at Castle, says today's aircraft pinups aren't so scantily clad as those of the 1940s. The sometimes-racy World War II pinups are "too sexist and not appropriate," he says.

"We want enthusiasm, vigor and spirit, but we don't want to offend anyone," says Martin.

Staff Sgt. Randy Jones says he found the model for the KC-135 painting on a 1943 calendar while browsing in Sonora, Calif. The calendar art was forwarded to base officials for review and approved by the previous wing commander.

From that, Staff Sgt. Ruben Rodriguez painted the aircraft's nose cone in nine hours during a routine inspection stop.

Plane art originated during World War I when aircraft first assumed a major role in warfare. The "Hat in The Ring Squadron" was among the best known pieces of plane art of the era and was emblazoned on the side of Capt. Eddie Rickenbacker's fighters.

During World War II, pinups such as "Ack Ack Annie," "Memphis Belle," "Pistol Packing Mama" and "Shoo Shoo Baby" were featured on warplanes and were considered a source of pride to the troops. But nose cones carried other art forms, such as "Blue Goos," and "Poop Deck Pappy."

Martin says he's already approved a sketch of a knight with a sword and shield mounted on a horse that will be painted on the nose of another Stratotanker. Jones says crews are continually looking for ways to personalize their planes, and they find nose cone art to be a perfect outlet.

"We paint the hubs but have to remove the paint when it is discovered," says Jones. "It's nice not to have to be sneaky."

AP Photo

Pinup art, popular on World War II fighter planes, is back. Staff Sgt. Randy Jones of Castle Air Force Base, Calif., found a 1943 calendar pinup as a model for the art on this KC-135 Stratotanker.

I WANT TO WRITE something beaut(i)ful
but I just don't know what i/t is.

and if I tell it like it (h)is,
who will ever publish (t)his?

or, if it is, will it be dis(miss)ed
as mere ravings of a feminist?

(and you could see it in their eyes
—how they'd pimp a few of the "poetess"'s works,
to keep her in the poet's "pen"
(that's as in baseball: "for the men")
in due course, they're serialized
(not in journals—merely "poetized")

      exercise *exercise*:

      pp. *exce-re* to drive on, keep busy
      fr. *ex-* + *arce-re* to enclose, hold off

      more at *ARK*

PARTING

The time has come to let it go,
The pain that's held my mind as vise,
Though who I am I do not know.

A certain fear—stepping free. What new road
Shall I plow if I leave behind the guise?
The time has come to let it go—

A blazing meteor—under waves mowed
To such sea-depths never will it rise.
Though who I am I do not know:

Here's the risk—green bay, uncharted, to row

Across, waves turned to lifting butterflies.

Across, waves turned to lifting butterflies.   *87*
The time has come to let it go

 That sad height and breathing depth that bowed
The song in flight like shattered railroad ties,
Though, who I was I do not know.

If it's true we wreak by what we sew,
And "no reason," for all the burning *why*'s,
The time has come to let it go,
Though who I'll be—
                                        I do not know.

but, of course,
the beat goes on

the beat goes on

cunt, whore, chick, bird, cheese
I ream,
     I dream,
          I cream,
               I scream,
                    I bream
(bare-beamed
bare-assed
bare-eyed)

Christmas with Morris and Boris
(more-"us"/ bore us):

Morris said,
"I will see him FIRST!"

"Get up! Get up!" they yelled.
"it is time to open your —-"

"I know," said Morris. "Our EYES!"

"No!" cried Boris. "They mean
it is time to open our —-"

"I know!" yelled Morris. Our MOUTHS! I see CANDY!"

. . .

Boris said,
"These are nice earmuffs."

Morris said,
"I can't HEAR you with them on.
You mean, HEARmuffs!"

(You mean HERmuffs! in a one-hearse-open-slay)

      Exercise sex-to-ate:

      retina:
      fr. L *rete* net
      akin to GK *ere-mos* l(one)ly
         sol(I)tary

      Exercise 6/9:

      retinal
      image

      retained
      re(s)trained

"You're standing on my foot."
Well, what foot, what feet,
what stand, what stance,
what stanza, what *verse*,

can for a woman be
stanza my stone?

Signing off,

Jacque Vaught Brogan
Professor
University of Notre Dame

[*professor*: der. fr. *profess*=to profess, to pretend, to confess—more at CONFESS]

[*university*: fr. L uni-versus]

... TO TRAVERSE THE UNIVERSE

x-star-I's s(eve)n-/:

star
iris

aster
i rise

Astarte (fr. Phoenician goddess of feritility
        and sexual love
asteria

Iris (1. rainbow: fr. goddess of the rainbow
        and messenger of the gods)
iris

iris diaphragm: an adjustable diaphragm
of thin opaque plates
that can be turned
by a (w)ring
so as to change
the diameter of a
central opening

Exercise 7 to 1:

irradiate (to cast rays of light upon)
irradiation (emission of radiant energy)

irrational
irradicable

Exercise 7/t(w)o:

the double meanings   of *rad(i)cal*—

of or *quarter*, or of *railroad*, or of *ties*, or of *revolution*
(not to mention rise of *evolution*—or of *ray* (fish, light, arrayed like a flower)

> *ANSWER*
> *ANOREXIA*
> *ANOXIA*
> *ANONYMO(US)*

"She needs to go to bed. You told me to listen
to her concerns. I listened—fuck it.
I can't do anything about it."

Really.
I've nothing more to say.

Who's got the last word?

banyans to bunyans
tell them it's not corn
(tell them it's *horn*"
tell them it hurts

HER/T/S

in Hawai'i
('i=island)

Kea-nuenue:
name of the god-

dess of the
rainbow.

When not a name,
written as

two words:
ke anue-

nue: the
rainbow

Makaha: prince
who betrayed
Kea-neuneue

(almost like
Pluto, leaving
withered valleys)

valley: more at VALE
vale: 1. more at VOLUBLE, valley, dale
vale: 2. more at WEILD

-[no *v*'s in Hawai'i:
wahahe'e: Liar]

(i'm losing wor(l)ds)
   already forgotten:
   lilinoe

         l(i)l(i)noe:
             f(i)ne m(i)st: ra(i)n

but (eve)n there: *mana—*
we've heard this before

man-a we've
He(a)rd this before

man(a): "Power possessed by man, but originating in the supernatural and thus imbued
with a m(y)stic quality"

(POWER possessed by MAN)

LOOK. LICK. LOCK. I'm not so happy.
hypo: 1. under: beneath: down
2. less than normal
3. in a lower state

Really. Don't get to know her. She's such a hypochondriac.

Ex-her-i's s*eve*n-tie th(r)ee:

goes like this:
hypocr(it)e: one who effects virtues
    (s)*he* does not have

hypo(e)ut(e)ctic: containing
    the minor component
    in an a-mount]

hyp(o)geal: [hipe the gals]=
    remaining below
    the ground
    while the
    epicotyl
    elongates

(I'm so frightened)

(1)*her.* MORE AT HE

(2)*her. objective case of* SHE

Hera: the queen of heaven
      sister and wife of Zeus   goddess of women and marriage

herald: more at HARRY/ WEILD
      [akin to OHG *heri*: army]

(Subverting the h[y]ms,]

REALLY. IT COULD BE ABOUT ANYTHING.
thing: akin to OHG *ding*; thing assembly. Goth: *the(i)s:*
    time

he (he-) pron. 2. Used to refer to any person whose sex is not specified.

[speci-c(i)zed]

he^2 (ha-) n. The 5th letter of the Hebrew alphabet
HE The symbol for the element helium

head

H bomb

A bomb

t(his) could make you entirely too heady
head mistress =/ head master

she (she-) pron. 2. Used traditionally of certain objects and institutions such as ships and nations.

Used traditionally
of certain objects

and institutions
such as ships and nations

Used. Traditionally.
of certain objects.
institutions.

    Exercise seventy(-)f(ea)r:

    Really,
    it's enough

    to make you
    scream

"Big girls don't cry." "I wanna be
Bobby's girl. I wanna be"

she (she-) n. A female animal or person: *a she-cat*

The Bettmann Archive

USAFTC, Library of Congress

"This is my rifle.
This is my gun.
The one is for shooting.
The other's for fun."

"How can I forget these lines?

how can (i) for?
get these l(i)nes?
these l(i)es

ta(l)king eyes

      X her i's s(e)v(e)n-(d)ive:

      in French:
      la belle chose

      the beaut(i)ful
      th(IN)g

ice pick, eyes pick, i's pick
prick= 2. to sting with a mental or emotional pang
(to prick up one's ears)
a prick in the conscience

women
wo+men

wo+hen
wo+him

+hym+0/
 hym+null
 =hymnal
boy inter. Used to express mild astonishment, elation, or disgust

girl
[gir(l)]
1. a female child who has not yet attained womanhood

(woman: hooded: veiled/Woman in Black)
2. a female child 3. an unmarried young woman
(by all etymolog(l)ies, a contra-diction *in terms,*
woman meaning wif-man)
4. a daughter
(T/HIS GETS REALLY FR(I)GHTEN(I)NG)

5. a sweetheart
(sw[ee]t her)
6. a female servant, employee, or clerk

girl Friday
girlhood
girlish
girly

one of the boys, the good ole' boys, the good old days
(Man in White. Woman in Black.)

Age 17: January 14, 1969

Little men in little purple suits,
Running around, playing their flutes,
Not caring what they are
Not even caring if near or far,
Living a contented complacent existence
Within the boundaries of their tiny fence.

Happy little men all of their lives.
Sad little men without any eyes.

ta(l)king eyes
tall king (i's)

and one from my Mother: "It is sheer good luck/ That always/ (Up to now, at least)/ The sun
returned/—And burned."

from the notebook, January 20, 1969:
now that he's gone
he is my mind

(gone to the dogs/gone in the language/ even then you could see she was a)

May 25, 1969:
 I write
of the only right
seen only in

"oh, i/t's just in her (i)mag(i)nat(i)on"

June 27, 1969

I'M NOT MAD—REALLY I'M NOT

Wistfully—oh how strange
is the wind
this evening. I feel deranged.
I can't mend
my mind. Crazy men
with their guns
and i with my pen

       exer-cease 7-sex::
       (i) knew i/t
       all
       along

August 6, 1969

anticipation/fell over the edge/and landed in my lap. lay there, looking up with lonely disappointed eyes. lost in its own pieces, it melted into a salty liquid rather like tears.

/why don't you just say so?/

August 16, 1969: The Eyes of My Room: Eyes haunt my room, Six pairs staring at me, Five refusing to look.

March 15, 1970: Words that Won't Come
There are words that won't come/for fear of being written/ but the thoughts are still there/ wandering in mind's air—and terribly aware.

"She's just a girl."

December 18, 1970:
melting eyes
What do you want me to realize?

January 8, 1968:
Often I've tried to write poetry
But the words have refused to come to me.
Time after time
The words would not rhyme,
But this one has worked out quite nicely.

/What language is she ta(l)king?/

September 1, 1968

faces
faces that suggest places
places where there were looks
looks that i mistook
mistook to be kindness
when they were only blindness
blindness caused by
faces

"What a face.
It's all in her face.
Get out of my face."

November 12, 1968:

—my true code—

November 8, 1974:

silver of your lonely eyes

April 22, 1975

you, who can see exactly what you wish
cannot understand me when my eyes are like sleeves
emptied of their arms
you, who can fill your thoughts as full as an egg (*eye* etymos)
cannot understand the hollow in my bones
the bowl between my arms

September 1975

a hole has no sense of its limits/ the visible measure of chaos/ the absense of nothingness/
telescoping blindly into me

December 1975
the moon glares more intensely/ than an interrogation light/it slaps me for/ confessions; it
flails at me/for guilt that would stain like the first/period/though i insist i did not mastermind
this world

          Exercise s(even)ty-heave(n):

          I insist
             (i) did not

          master/
          mind

          t/his
          wor(l)d

[]
][

ta(l)king eyes

it/s all in her m(i)nd

she just up & went crazy

isn't that just like a woman

(no justice: just "us")

   x or sighs: 78

   try th(ink)
   -ing about

   something
   e(l)se

so I can't write in this language
but I want it to be more
than "rev(i)s(i)onist poetry
still, it is funny the five interpretations—and how women "inter-pret" while men "unpack"
(i)deas—should I ever write:

my master's eyes are nothing like the sun

and what it means if his feet tread the ground

and he: (as a stateMENt of roMANce):

   Be the voice of night and Florida in my ear.
   Use dusky words and dusky images.
   Darken you speech.

   Speak, even, as if I did not hear you speaking,
   But spoke for you perfectly in my thoughts,
   Conceiving words.

Do not go gentle under that good knight.

Rage, rage, against the dying of your sight.

Exerc(ai)se: seve(n-)ty none:

like a living doll!

the mirror image
the spitting image

You're 1969 poetry is not so interesting.
But you're 1975 is devestating.
I can't remember. Oh, the moon as interrogation lamp.
Yes. Or the eyes as sleeves.
That too

At least you could look at me when I'm talking.

It's white hot, the pain [pa(i)n: pa/in]. Like a cultural angst, a particular feminine pain.
And I couldn't talk to my mother. And I didn't want to talk to my father—you know how
he was talking.

Burning. White hot. I can't begin to tell you the pain.
....

Feeling better?

Metaphysical exfolitation.

You look so cheerful.
Where's the empathy?

em(path)y

now you're doing it too

it's horrible

ta(l)king eyes

iknowthat'sthe point

not to mention em (cognate *in*, assimilated to *p*) +
    pa + thy

        right

"though it may look like (*write* it!) like disaster"
dis/aster

titles (as revelation):

Peter Quince at the Clavier
The Silver Pough-Boy
The Death of a Soldier
Le Monocle de Mon Oncle
The Man Whose Pharynx Was Bad
The Doctor of Geneva
The Snow Man The Comedian as the Letter C
The Emperor of Ice-Cream
Anecdote of the Prince of Peacocks
The Brave Man
The Men That Are Falling
The Man on the Dump
The Latest Freed Man
The Sense of the Sleight-of-Hand Man
Man and Bottle
Man Carrying Thing

Large Red Man Reading

An Old Man Asleep

(not to mention:
For an Old Woman in a Wig
The Plot against the Giant
The Paltry Nude Starts on a Spring Voyage
Infanta Marina
Another Weeping Woman

A High-Toned Old Christian Woman
The Virgin Carrying a Lantern
United Dames of America
So-And-So Reclining on Her Couch

A Pastoral Nun

Madame La Fleurie
Good Man. Bad Woman.

The Pure Good of Theory: quoth the noble
baron burns: I have a prejudice against. . . .

"anywhere between 10 and 20 thousand for a healthy white. . .
of course if you want one of those [black
or bi-racial] $400"

you'd think it would be against the law

yes (she said) you'd think so/ th(ink) sew

what to do with all this pain
it's burning, like a brand, right through my heart
i go outside. i wish for rain.

 they'd frame the sheets to show her stain
(in a nunnery, after she did her part)
and what can i do with all this pain?

no words that aren't against the grain
confess: disfigured madonna eat your heart
out (i go outside. i wish for rain.)

it's truly everywhere—this stain—
against half the human race—the part
that carries *can i do with all this pain?*

it's just like going on a train
(the railroad ties I didn't mark)
and all our efforts all in vain—

if we could find i/t in the brain
and make as gifts (not commerce) of such art,
i'd know what to do with all this pain:
i'd go outside. and wait for rain.

Tell her to shut up.
I don't want to hear her anymore.

Why won't she mind?

(a question accused/asked specifically against/of girls)

excavating the self/releasing the repressions/such danger
excavate: < L. ex /out/ cavare make hollow /carve/

exactly! (look that one up yourself)

/naturally, derives from AGENT: "a person responsible for
                                    HIS acts"

Exercise 7 (sex):

man: explodes
woman: implodes

This Poem Has Me Possessed

and my father didn't even write me back
[anger , fr. strangle]

really, and women strang(l)ed the w(hole) wor(l)d round

syn IRE, RAGE, FURY, INDIGNATION, WRATH: ANGER is the general term for the emotional reaction of extreme displeasure and suggests neither a definite degree of intensity nor a necessarily outward manifestation; IRE is now chiefly literary and suggests great intenstity and its exhibition in acts or words; RAGE implies loss of self-control from violence of emotion; FURY suggests even more violence and connotes a degree of temporary madness; INDIGNATION stresses righteous anger at what one considers unfair, mean, or shameful; WRATH may imply either rage or idignation but suggests strongly a desire or intent to avenge or plumb

]of course: women de-scribed as the Furies all along. but it was IRE (re/pressed), and INDIGNATION [and in-dig-nation]

men JAM and then UNPACK
(women never can be infuriated/only infibulated)

INDIGNANT: < unworthy (MORE AT DECENT)

(decent 1b: HANDSOME)

trying to get the big picture
(but I think we did this before: *big*=important man)

and, if in language, *big* is man, what's *small*
[*etymos*: *bad*]

[i th(ink)
i'll just

ta(l)king eyes

just variant of JOUST

just right/law

just exactly, precisely

i just need to exercise

[god is gracious + pretty/light grace small shoes/trousers]

sticks and stones may break my bones
but words will never hurt me

E(cores)I's 8/0:

false
fallatious

fallatio
    felatio
        phallus
(foul us)

A rose by any other name
would smell as sweet.

[and, *of course,*
at NOTRE DAME—

the fight song!
(only brothers)

NB: what's the *fe-* to female anyway
(not, *of course,* in the dictionary)

Note: *feal* (more at faith)
and   *fear* (more at danger)

(see FARE)
and never (FAIR)

{fare: to eat, as a man always does
fair: to decorate, as a woman always does}

[fibula: a clasp resembling a safety pin used by the ancient Greeks and Romans]

decorate:
more at ADORN

adorn:
more at ORNATE
ornate:
more at ORDAIN

ordain:
more at ABIDE, DEAL

deal: < OHG *tell* (or part)

what despair, what language, what anguish where
the *me* disappears, for the I that continually comes and goes

go: (for a man)=Gk. to attain
[for wo-men= *go away*; re-st(r)ain)]

No-name/no-nom/no-plume
[no flame/ non "on"/ no fume]

Exercise eighty (i)t:

in the blink of an eye

(he got her
dead in the eye)

movie: —the rape of the eye—

(most female/wo-men doctors=
knowing eyes)

WHY DON'T YOU JUST SHUT UP
AND TAKE IT LIKE

JUST GRIT YOUR TEETH
AND TAKE IT LIKE A

a mere note: *rape/radish* <akin to turnip
    and more at ROOT=
        [in ME and OE: *wroten*]

so (sew) *he wrote on her*
[*tattoo*: an indelible mar/
k or figure
(fuck/her) fixed
upon the body by insertion
of a pig-
MENt or by the produc-
tion (SHUN) of scars]

scar: =shear/ scabbard/ score

    "if you tell anyone, I'll"

/If she tells he'll scar her daughter.
If she tells he'll tell her son.
If she tells it means more slaughter.
Either way, he's a(l)ways won.

Exercise nun eighty two:

or SO/SEW they tell us
(which is why we chose this course)

 mental/ infibulation:
we wonder which is worse

or MENtal)e/ in FIB-U-(e)lation:
exactly why women curse

 . . . and really, it's just got to be a joke (note: merely the voiced fricative of *choke*)—
dictionaries must be written by men—how else this:?

scarfpin: TIEPIN
(so absurd: when everyone knows the TIE means *see my head (the one up) see my head
(points down)/* whereas SCARFPIN is more exactly *scar/pen* or *tie me up, bind me, fuck
me*

(the actual etmology is: *sling*)

LIKE A FLOWER

Like a flower, opening, I sing to you
the way an iris opens to the dark.
All is not lost—it's like an early lark
singing (finally) morning's lifting hue:

black embraces pink—orange, gold,—and blue
like a mother's arm, or raising of the ark
above the haggard mountains (clear, and stark—
such places I have wandered, as if a Jew):

meaning: outcast, silenced, given to a queue
meaning: branded, then made to wear the mark
(or as scarlet letter: *their* "re-mark"
that made "I" a mere inversion of "you").

Not a *Divine Comedy*: yet i rise
as if from Purgatory—opening eyes.

(like a flower, petals opening
one by one
separate, drawn
by Spirit, not by force
rising, where we mingle
light infused

[no *force that through the green fuse drives the flower*
no *I am the torpedo/ you the cave*—

ocillating/scintillating fingers
spreading out—
they touch the tone
before eye hears the word

wavings, as if unmeasured,
—desired—
/"ethical 'not-yet'"/
exactly like each rainbow's arch

(a perfect cirle from the plane/
a sweeping parabola, at her birth/
several, "marching" down the valley/
so close, I could stick my hand
    right through
    (*write* through)

it looked like (*write* it !) like an aster

x-H/E/R/ (i) 83:

asters should flower

and women's fingers—

if (s)he were ever heard

this may be the last time. this may be the last time. this may be the last time. i don't know
(i don't know)

manipulation=infibulation=ejaculation +
hysteria=uterus

hi'story: is that so intelligent? is that smart? what would PLATO do?
 APOLOGIZE?
(punch her in the eye)

all the lives
(I)'ve k(no)n

say Jesse
I'm lonely come home

Exercise LXXXIV:

iris opens
and closes

responsive
to the light

whether rainbow,
flower, or

the eye

in Greek, *o-ps* meant *eye* and *face*
(for only half the human race
the rest priapistically erased)

    he said, you'd better not read the two-
    volume anthropology /*anthropology*:

      1)the science of man;
esp: the study of man
in relation to the distribution,
origin, classification, and relationship
of races, physical character, environmen-
tal and social relations, and culture

      2)teaching
about the origin,
nature and destiny of man,
especially from the perspective
of his
relation to God

    he said: infibulation is only the beginning

)i knew t/he/y wrote the book(

ta(l)king eyes

it's all in her looks

ta(l)king eyes

Manuscript page:

voiced	/	unvoiced:
voiced		foist
vane/vain		feign
buy		pie
boy		poi
joke		choke
die		tie
talking aye's		ta(l)king eyes
I		(())

ta(l)king eyes

(eye) have an I
when   you see   us
(yes) women
then shall we re(l)ease you, eye to I

****

sonnet: no rhyme nor reason

When I look with
time—like, childhood greening—
my own irises
closely, it is as if with wonder

(though it's true I never
see them together
though I try)
that I seee each one

pulsing, con-
tracting, opening
line, changing like sun's
rays at eye of dawn

of dawn of eve: at deepest
blue, such yellow

****

found son/
        net

he robbed me blind
            still eye consistently
assert a few pulses or anga-
                    grams
—shall innocence grow until i die
(dredging up all the way the scars
                    the slime)?

where is the i?
        —printer—
                say differently
(we kNOw such grand achieveMENts
                on his terms:
we know the veils
        —his scanning eyes—
repeating, re-
        peating what we should (l)earn:

fuck her brains out   eyes
            write between the
{wanting light to write me back from be-
                    yond}
——i pull myself to the mirror
                rites of eye
the moist mar(k)ed image
                still
                    bringing me home:
then shall I fly (when child
            (hood) is not
nostalgia, not love, not fearing subject

****

DEAR PETER—

There are many ways of responding
—re/sounding—take this
as the compliment
and complement
I intend.

                    Jacque

P. S. No doubt: anyone reading this
will conlcude I don't
like sex—or at least
the opposite sex.
                    Please
be prepared to testi-
fy "that's not it/
not it at all."

****

hope is voice of future
rewriting
writing over
riding a/
cross such (vo)i(d)

                    May 20, 2008

            —and for whom—
and how the pain attacks my heart
—i feel the welling,

the prolapsing,   it looks like
contractions

of
or any other orifice

    (or)i(face)

hell: we can *reverse* the line
(woman in white/ man in black—
)
and it doesn't change a thing:

just continuing sacrifices
for the few allowed in

       exercise ate/s(h)even:

       sacrifice
       orifice
       scarify

       sacrifice:
       <L *sacer*: holy/cursed
       MORE AT SCARED

         1. the offering of an immolated victim
         2. to sell at a loss
         3. to make a scarifice hit in baseball

and look at t/his: these things
just find me

       Why they've erased
       the woman.

I know. And *this* is
woman in white/ man in black and
it doesn't change a thing.

Only Part Of The Picture.

the whole picture

. . . and look at *t/his*: it's her
story/ her
version/ but it's like

IN THE WAITING ROOM:

"If what we see could forget us
half as easily," I want to tell you.

and another: "I left because I was lost
I was running to my life
You see, i/t seemed to be slipping through
my fingers/ I was losing myself.

t/he/y felt they had *created*
me," she added. I felt
they'd *discovered* me.
There's a difference.

I felt like a piece
of merchandise.

       (sum) exercise:

       merchandise:
       marred
           (hand)
        eyes

"T/he/ir attitude was: 'Don't let her talk.
The glamour gowns work, just cover
her up in clothes."
"

ta(l)king eyes

All I wanted was for t/hem to
tell me I was
doing something right"

finally, I have to write

"or let me find some way that I . . . ."

AND WHY WE CANNOT SPEAK/ WHY WE'RE NEVER HEARD:

Para-exercise:

Forgetting your face / I
still recall / the text/
of your narrow shoulder

read by my fingertips

OR

you in blue
in morning light
(through such
square panes/pains)

OR

you
still naked
inside
your clothes

OR

we separated
while the eye
sets, the
sun blinks

OR

or how about
(I'll be damned)   *this*: Diamorphic

We are not the same.   Mine's the primordial short count.
Soaring on clipped wings.
You are at home.
Where the housefly rests.

and *that* t(he)y say is poetry

///
finding my buried
self—
it's like old poems

in a closed
note-
book//

Exercise: (sum) unknown number:

in the bl(ink) of an eye

in the w(ink) of an eye

st(ink) eye:-

evil (i)

deviled eggs/ deviled ojos/ deviled eyes

]one month's meditation
and all the apsects
of a period

ta(l)king eyes

cycles of the moon
moon/menses/lunacy

time to get on with my life
to finish this manuscript
—developed logophobia: actually afraid of *manuscript*:

man <L. hand
as is manual—as in labor—
as is manual—as in pre/scriptive book

as is manner (meaning in the ways of men)
[ergo: literally impossible to say "in the *manner* of women"

as is manuscript

nothing eye-catching, but it's in his hands

—and to get on with what i'm supposed to be writing

(what i'm sup-
posed
to be

writing
in some language
i do not

prec(is)ely
not the same
category

man of the hour/Lady Day/ man of the night=/ lady of the night

Exhereyes:

Look at th/his:
words say me

while ra(is)ing
you: a one-

way mirror
(w/her/e i see

you behind
every word—

 —com-
posing

my sentences
with ta(l)king eyes

s(i)gned,
sincerely yours,

just another
a/not/her
telling lies

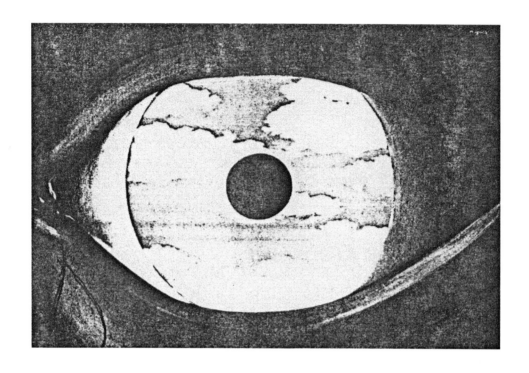

Guide to Images, Postcards, and Clippings from the Author's Collection, gathered during the time of writing this book

Note on the Author

Jacque Vaught Brogan is a poet, scholar, and Professor at the University of Notre Dame. Her poems have appeared in such journals as *The Women's Studies Journal, The Wallace Stevens Journal, The Formalist, HOW(ever), Poetry International, Kalliope, Hubbub, Boundary 2, Connotations, Continuum, Connecticut Poetry Review*; and in *The Anthology of New England Poets*. She has authored several critical books on American poetry and numerous essays on American poetry, fiction, and theory. She also co-edited (with Cordelia Candelaria) *Women Poets of the Americas: Toward a Pan-American Gathering*, and co-edited (with Albert Gelpi) a special issue of *The Women's Studies Journal* devoted to the more recent work of Adrienne Rich. She has been the featured poet in *Connotations, Spring*, and *Poetry International*. Her previous book of poetry, *Damage*, includes a final section called "Notes from the Body" which is the most immediate precursor to *ta(l)king eyes*. She has two adult children, Jessica and Evan, both graduates of Notre Dame.

Chax Press

Chax Press programs and publications are supported by donations from individuals and foundations, as well as from the Tucson Pima Arts Council and the Arizona Commission on the Arts, with funding from the State of Arizona and the National Endowment for the Arts.

Arizona
Commission
on the Arts

NATIONAL
ENDOWMENT
FOR THE ARTS

TUCSON PIMA
ARTS
COUNCIL

Other Books from Chax Press

CA Conrad, *The Book of Frank*

Michael Cross, *In Felt Treeling: A Libretto*

Patrick Pritchett, *Salt, My Love: A Ballad*

Jeanne Heuving, *Transducer*

John Tritica, *Sound Remains*

Elizabeth Treadwell, *Wardolly*

Karen Mac Cormack, *Implexures* (complete edition)

Steve McCaffery, *Slightly Left of Thinking*

Beth Joselow, *Begin at Once*

David Abel, *Black Valentine*

Hilton Obenzinger, *Busy Dying*

Linh Dinh, *Jam Alerts*

Leonard Schwartz, *A Message Back and Other Furors*

Linda Russo, *Mirth*

Frances Sjoberg, *Outcrop*

Beverly Dahlen, *A-Reading Spicer & 18 Sonnets*

Jefferson Carter, *Sentimental Blue*

Keith Wilsoon, *Transcendental Studies*

Bruce Andrews, *Swoon Noir*

Eli Goldblatt, *Speech Acts*

Norman Fischer, *Slowly but Dearly*

Gil Ott, *Traffic*

Jerome Rothenberg, *A Book of Concealments*

Nick Piombino, *Hegelian Haiku*

Nathaniel Mackey, *Four for Glenn*

Hank Lazer, *Deathwatch for My Father*

and many more. Please visit our web site at http://chax.org.